To Mally –
For many happy
hours collecting
Jackie

11-11-89

To Mally –
With best wishes –
Anne Day Smith

Anne Day Smith
Jacqueline Andrews

Limited
Collector's
Edition
1114 of 2400

The Andrews Collection:

Personal Treasures

by Anne Day Smith

The Andrews Collection:

Personal Treasures

by Anne Day Smith

Dee's Delights, Inc., Cincinnati, Ohio

Acknowledgments

The author wishes to acknowledge and thank the following people who have been an integral part of this project:

Jacqueline Hammond Andrews, whose collection is the subject of this book, a genuine Southern lady whose warmth, vitality, and sense of humor have made this project a most enjoyable and enlightening experience.

H. Augustus Miller, whose excellent photographs of the collection have added a vital dimension to the book.

Beverly Keeton, our assistant during the photography sessions, whose knowledge of the collection was invaluable.

And, as always, my special thanks to Gerry, without whose guidance and insight, love and support, I could not have completed this project.

Copyright © 1988 by Anne Day Smith
ISBN 0-938685-04-X (Hardcover) 0-938685-05-8 (Softcover)
BOY760 (Hardcover) BOY137 (Softcover)
All rights reserved. No portion of this book may be reproduced in any form without the written permission of the publisher, Dee's Delights, Inc., 3150 State Line Rd, (Cincinnati) North Bend, OH 45052.

Editing and art production by Deanna Hacker.
Typesetting by Jacqueline Young Enterprises.
Printed in the United States of America.

All photographs are by Anne Day Smith with the exception of the following, which were taken by Gus Miller: pgs. 10, 11, 12, 13, 20, 24, 28, 33, 34 (upper), 36, 37, 38, 39, 42, 43, 60, 62, 63, 64, 68, 80, 83 (upper), and 97.

The photographs on pages 32 and 96 were provided by Jackie Andrews.

All of the quotations used in this book are in the public domain. In the captions under the photographs, we have tried to be as accurate as possible in identifying the craftsmen or artisans who made many of the items shown. As in any collection, especially one of this size, it is not always possible to identify every item, and we sincerely apologize for any errors or omissions.

On the cover: Victorian doll house by Ron and April Gill. Three bisque collector dolls — left, an early E. Jumeau; center, a French mechanical doll; right, a Tête Jumeau. Oriental bed by Hermania Anslinger.

For Chip, Rick and Stephen

and

For Jill, Cecile, Joe Jr., Bill and John

The "collections" we are most proud of.

A selection of teddy bears, both old and new, both hand-made and commercial, sit in a chair with a woven rush seat that Jackie used when she was a child.

Contents

These two antique composition dolls are from the Andrews Collection.

This woodworking shop was built by John Powers. Other tools are by Paul Darrah.

Introduction

A collection of your own is as unique as a fingerprint, as personal as a family album. Whether it takes you ten minutes or ten years to acquire the items that comprise it, your collection makes a statement about you, what you admire, what you treasure, what you personally find interesting.

There is no typical collector. Our collections are as diverse as we ourselves. Some of us are reluctant to explain why we collect what we do and prefer to keep our collections private. Others, like Jacqueline Hammond Andrews, believe that the very best way to enjoy their collections is to share them.

Here, for your enjoyment, are many of the personal treasures of this very special lady.

From the playthings of the past to the work of today's artisans, the Andrews Collection is remarkable in its diversity. The collection, acquired over the past quarter century, fills to overflowing a 2,500-square-foot space.

There are more than 200 dolls ranging in size from over two feet tall down to only two inches tall. The fifty or so teddy bears and other animals range in age from the mid-nineteenth century to the present. Many of the dolls and animals sit on doll- and sample-size furniture, child-size toys, or fill a baby's cradle.

Jackie Andrews has collected the work of a wide variety of miniatures artisans and craftsmen throughout the past twenty-five years. She has compiled a unique record of their development and growth, from their beginnings as novice craftsmen to the perfection they have now achieved in their chosen mediums.

The miniatures collection contains almost fifty significant structures, ranging in type from a one-inch-scale church to a half-inch-scale dollhouse. The largest is a sixteen-foot-long southern plantation. Nestled between them are fifty smaller buildings of various types. There are over thirty-five decorated room boxes and twenty free-standing displays such as domes, plus an uncounted array of individual items.

Throughout these pages you will have an in-depth look at a collection that is an important contribution and tribute to the hobby of collecting miniatures, antique toys and dolls. It encompasses the old and the new, the large and the small — the special treasures of one truly unique collector.

Welcome To The Andrews Collection

Jackie Andrews

Ah, to build, to build!
That is the noblest of all the arts.
—Henry Wadsworth Longfellow

Carter's Grove* 🏠

The miniature replica of Carter's Grove Plantation, near Williamsburg, Virginia, is by far the largest dollhouse in the Andrews Collection. It is sixteen feet nine inches long, including the two wings at either end.

The miniature Carter's Grove was commissioned by Betty Carter Marvin, a descendant of Robert "King" Carter, the original landowner of Carter's Grove Plantation. The replica was built by Dr. Charles E. Holcomb of Hendersonville, North Carolina, during the period from 1980 to 1984. Dr. Holcomb spent 2,700 hours working on the 35-room house.

When Mrs. Marvin commissioned the replica of Carter's Grove, she intended it as a gift to the Colonial Williamsburg Foundation and had received permission to allow the builder and other artisans to visit the real Carter's Grove to take measurements and make scaled drawings of everything that would be needed to create the miniature.

During the period when the dollhouse

was being built, Jackie was aware of its existence, of course. "I had jokingly said to Betty," she recalls, "that if Williamsburg didn't want it, I'd take it. She had bought some things from us, and I had seen two pieces of the house which I just fell in love with." Still, Jackie was unprepared when she received Betty's phone call one late December afternoon, suggesting that if the Andrewses still wanted the dollhouse they should meet her at the builder's home two days later. The original arrangement with the Colonial Williamsburg Foundation had fallen through.

"So Joe and I went, in the worst sleet storm I ever saw," Jackie continued, "up the mountain to the builder's house, to meet Betty and see the dollhouse. The whole time we were there looking at the house, Dr. Holcomb was going outdoors, feeling the asphalt driveway to be sure it wasn't freezing because he didn't want us all up there as house guests." Joe and Jackie Andrews agreed to buy the house and

Carter's Grove is a trademark owned by the Colonial Williamsburg Foundation.

took possession of it the following spring, in May 1984.

Even though the house is over sixteen feet long, it can be moved because it comes apart in sections. "The end wings are separate," Jackie explains, "the middle wings are separate, the chimneys come off, and the main house divides down the center. But, it's so well done that you cannot tell, inside or out, unless you really look for the seams."

The house came to Jackie partly furnished, and she is still working on several of the main rooms of the house to complete the furnishings. "The big house is done today with a lot of Victorian, and this one has Victorian in it, but I'm doing away with that," she comments. "I'm just imagining that a young couple has bought it, and they are using some attic furniture and slowly buying antiques." Jackie made all the window treatments and re-painted the walls and woodwork in several rooms.

Among the furnishings Jackie received with the house were an unusual number of brass candlesticks. "I counted them the last time I cleaned them; there were ninety-eight," she comments. Cleaning the components of a dollhouse like Carter's Grove is not an easy process, but Jackie has the help of a unique device when it comes to cleaning the brass: she uses a tumbler.

"I bought mine at the gun shop," she confides. "It's used to polish the brass bullets. It uses ground walnut hulls, and you just put the pieces in there and let it run three to four hours, take them out, and they are beautiful. You can't put a whole lot in it, but I can do a room or two at a time," she continues. The machine costs twenty-five dollars, "but I wouldn't take anything for it," Jackie insists, because of the time it saves her.

Like many houses with long, interesting histories, the real Carter's Grove is purported to have a ghost in residence, and Jackie is convinced that a miniature one lives in her Carter's Grove. "He lives in one of the upper rooms on the land side of the real house," she remarks, "but he lives downstairs in my house, and he doesn't let you see him, he runs." She demonstrates by opening the side of the house to expose the dining room, and as she does so, the door between the dining room and hall quickly swings open and then shut. "It happens," Jackie insists, "no matter what other

These views of Carter's Grove show the house from the more formal, or river, side. The actual house faces the James River.

doors are open in the rest of the house. I'm convinced," she laughs.

"Lots of people," Jackie adds, "have wanted to know if Carter's Grove was mortgaged," as Wilton, an earlier acquisition, had been, but it was not. If it had been, the mortgage would have been substantially larger than her first one, and as Jackie says, "One mortgage was enough." Mortgage or not, the miniature replica of Carter's Grove Plantation is a priceless treasure in the Andrews Collection.

Carter's Grove has a sophisticated electrical system, providing a variety of lighting elements to individual rooms.

Betty Valentine created the wing chairs and one of the side chairs for this elegant library. She also made both the sofas which are copies of the ones that are in the Governor's Palace in Williamsburg. The desk is by E. M. Willits, and the corner chair by Helen Dorsett. Randy Himes built the two side tables, which were Houseparty favors in 1985. Glassware is by Francis Whittemore, and the sculpture on the desk is by Mary McGrath. Allen Martin built the bookcases, and Joe Andrews made the rug, using a transfer process.

The dining room (above) contains a sideboard and chairs by Andrews Miniatures, a tea caddy and cellarette by R. Simms, and silver by Kupjack and Cini. The andirons were created by Chet Spacher.

An elegant desk by Julian Biggers stands in the corner of the room that is known as the Refusal Room. Nellie Belt made the sofa and Carol Hardy created the tea table.

Edward Norton created the Windsor chairs around a unique wine-tasting table in this room, which served as the plantation office. Chet Spacher made the candlesticks, one of which the resident "ghost" of Carter's Grove seems to have knocked over.

All of the cupboards in this butler's pantry have doors that open to reveal shelves, and every drawer is functional as well. Much of the food in this room was created by Sylvia Clark. Gail Wise made the basket of peaches, and the black doll on the right was created by Susan Sirkis. The demijohns came from Albert's Glass.

In this room, known as the Old Kitchen, the table has two dowels extending from each end under the table top. These were used for hanging freshly made noodles to dry. Warren Dick made the bench and spinning wheel, and there are seventeen flat irons lined up on the mantel. Chet Spacher made the brass tea pot on stand.

The table, made by M. Brown in 1983, is a copy of the one in the corresponding room in the real Carter's Grove. Pottery in this room was made by Jim Clark, Jane Graber, and Deborah McKnight. Chet Spacher made the scales.

Jackie dressed the bed and made the draperies in this room. Dorothy Midgett painted the Warren Dick highboy on the back wall. Other Warren Dick pieces in the room include a tea table, lowboy, cradle, and chaise. The chest at the foot of the bed is by L. L. Cutright, and Gerald Crawford created the shaving stand. The desk in the niche on the left is by Joe Murter, with a chair by Delores Rawding. Susan Sirkis created both the dolls in this room. The one next to the bed is her first miniature doll.

Hermania Anslinger created this unusual bed. Dorothy Midgett handpainted the highboy, and Jackie created the wing chair using legs carved for her by Gerald Crawford. The chair's upholstery matches the draperies in this room.

This bedroom (left) contains several pieces of furniture from Gerald Crawford's Winterthur Collection. Betty Valentine made the wing chair, and the crewelwork on the bed was done by Pamela Andrews, Jackie's daughter-in-law. Chet Spacher made the andirons, and the bed warmer is by Frances Steak.

**The bed has become a place of luxury to me!
I would not exchange it for all the thrones in the world.**
—*Napoleon Bonaparte*

Dolls Were Her First Love

There are over 200 dolls in Jackie's collection.

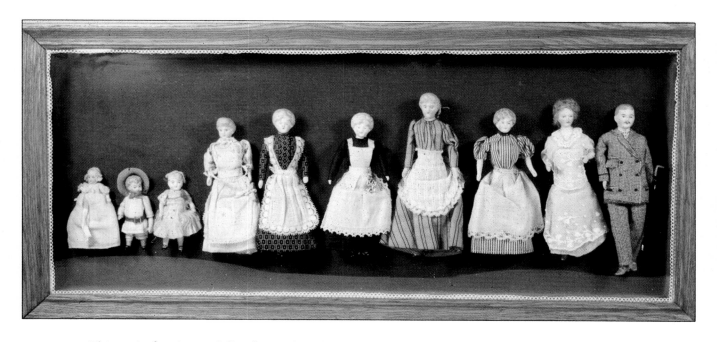

This set of antique dolls, framed under glass, are dressed in their original costumes.

The antique Bye-lo doll on the right is four inches tall. The three baby dolls nestled in its lap are English, and the child doll on the left is German. The porcelain doll in its lap was created by Martha Farnsworth. The baby layette shown here was stitched by Patti Highfill. Bye-lo baby dolls were first created in the early 1920s by Grace Storey Putnam, an art teacher who set out to create a doll that was completely realistic, using newborn babies in a Los Angeles hospital as her models.

"Dinah," the cloth doll in this photograph, was made in Ashland, Virginia, about 1900 by a Miss Annie Kenningham, according to the handwritten provenance attached to her petticoat. The large doll next to her is a Greiner, dated 1858. In front, from left to right, are a boy doll, origin unknown, an F. G. fashion doll with her original costume, a Parian, and a Steiner. The tiny doll dressed in pink is a Wink Eye Boy by Heubach.

A selection of dolls from around the world. The fabric doll on the left is East Indian, and next to her are the Rotherberg whistling children from Germany. On the right are Lord Krishna and his lady, both made of fabric. The seated doll on the left is a celluloid doll from Austria, and the one on the right is marked "Western Germany, U.S. Zone." The tiniest doll in this photograph has a wire body covered with fabric.

Backward, turn backward, O Time, in your flight,
Make me a child again just for tonight.

—*Elizabeth Akers Allen*

A tin autobus provides the background for an assortment of teddy bears and other animals. The red wagon is metal with rubber wheels and is marked "Radio Flyer USA." The bear in the wagon is a Steiff, as are several of the others. The monkey was also probably made in Germany.

These toys are mostly celluloid, but the cart and the stump the monkey is sitting on are tin. The cart toy and the horse toy are both marked "Made in Japan."

These colorful tin toys were made in the United States and Japan.

23

Jackie and Joe

Jackie Andrews

If you believe that collectors are born and not made, then you must also believe Jackie Andrews' assertion that "I never grew up." She did, of course, but only in the literal sense. The collection she has put together over the last quarter of a century reflects her enthusiasm for, and dedication to, the child that exists in all of us. It also reflects her personal resolve to pass on a legacy to future generations, to show the playthings of yesterday and the collectibles of today so that others, too, may not have to "grow up."

Jacqueline Hammond Andrews was born and raised in Ashland, Virginia, where she still lives. Ashland was a resort and mineral spring community one hundred and twenty-five years ago, built along the tracks of the Richmond, Fredericksburg and Potomac Railroad. Now the streets beside the train tracks are a restored historical area with shops and other businesses lining both sides.

There are four generations of Jackie's family living in Ashland today, and the town is best known as the home of Randolph-Macon College, which was founded after the Civil War. Joe Andrews, from Pittsburgh, Pennsylvania, was a student at Randolph-Macon, majoring in chemistry, when he and Jackie met. "There were about twelve of us girls of dating age,"

Jackie tells us, her inimitable Southern drawl stretching the word *there* to *they-ah* and dropping the *g* from the endings of some words, "and three hundred nineteen young men in college, with no cars." Jackie and her high school friends often went to the local drug store to have lunch and to watch the young men come to collect their mail at the post office next door. "We knew exactly where to hang out," she smiles mischievously.

A mutual friend introduced Joe and Jackie, and they started dating while she was still in high school. The September after she graduated, Jackie Hammond enrolled at Stratford, a college for women in Danville, Virginia, but she stayed there just short of a full school year because in April, she and Joe were quietly married in a small Methodist church in Danville. When the school found out about the marriage, "they packed me up and shipped me home," Jackie remembers. "You didn't stay in school married. They got me out of there in nothing flat."

Jackie's parents took her home, and, she continues, "they wanted to get a lawyer and have it annulled, and I said, 'Have it annulled if you want to, but I'll marry him again.' It'll be fifty years this April (1989), and it's been great," she confirms with a smile.

The newlyweds lived at first with Jackie's parents at Lakeview Farm on the outskirts of Ashland, and then moved to a place of their own about a year later when their first child, Jill, was born. Joe first worked for a tobacco company, and then was with General Electric for the next seventeen years. During those years, the Andrews had four more children, Cecile, Joe Jr., Bill and John. The large Victorian house the family lived in during those years was a busy place, indeed.

When Joe left General Electric, he and Jackie bought a small department store in Ashland, D. B. Cox & Company, which they ran until the early 1960s, when new shopping centers began to take business away from stores in the center of town. After their store closed, Joe managed finances for a local stained-glass company for a number of years. Later, in 1968, Jackie applied for what she thought would be a two-week job at the Randolph-Macon College infirmary. After twenty years, she is still there.

"The only credentials I had were that I had raised five children and helped at the birth of two others for one of our local doctors who was also a physician at the college," Jackie explains. "Each of them was born and I had them laying up on their mother's tummy before the doctor even arrived," she continues. "It was the thrill of a lifetime, when there are only two of you in the room, and suddenly there is a third person."

With that experience, Jackie was hired as night supervisor for the college infirmary, and she and Joe moved into a campus apartment next door. It was just a few years earlier that Jackie began what would become an extensive collection of dolls, miniatures and toys.

"I was helping a friend of mine here in town clean out one of these old Victorian houses that the family had lived in forever," Jackie remembers. A dumpster sat outside to collect whatever would be thrown away. Jackie's three-year-old son, John, was playing in the back yard while the two women sorted and packed household furnishings. "He got quiet, so I went to look for him," she continues. "He had crawled into the dumpster, and that's when I found the dolls." Besides John, the dumpster contained half a dozen antique bisque dolls. "I had never seen an antique doll; I didn't know what they were, but I hauled them home."

Jackie began to research and repair the dolls, and as she did, her interest grew. She acquired almost three hundred dolls, as well as doll furniture, carriages and sets of doll dishes over the next few years. She also repaired dolls for other collectors and had a small museum where she could display her own collection. She became an active member of the United Federation of Doll Clubs (U.F.D.C.) through the Dollology Club in Washington, D. C. During this time, she also acquired the first dollhouse in her collection, a miniature replica of Lakeview Farm, in 1966. It was built by a close friend of the Andrewses and remains her favorite house today.

Several years later, Jackie built a dollhouse herself. Called the miller's house, it is a copy of the building at Rockett Mill not far from Ashland, built in 1735 as a general store and post office for the surrounding area. The miniature replica was a blue ribbon prize winner when it was displayed at a U.F.D.C. regional convention in Williamsburg, Virginia, in 1971.

It was in connection with the convention that Jackie decided she was interested in miniatures not only as a hobby, but also as a business. She had been asked to design a table centerpiece for the convention. "I don't think the centerpiece ever materialized," Jackie recalls now, "but that's when the handbag developed."

Jackie had sketched a house based on the dormered center section of the Brush-Everard House in Colonial Williamsburg, showed it to Joe, and said, "I want a handbag and I want it this big, and he said, 'That means absolutely nothing to me,' " as Jackie recalls the conversation today. Although Joe was well acquainted with woodworking and had built many pieces of furniture for their home, he wanted something more substantial than Jackie's sketch before he tried to build the handbag from wood.

"So, I went to the book store," Jackie continues, "and there on the floor was a box that books had come in, with the top slanted, and I said to myself, 'That's the size house I need.' I brought it home and gave it to him." Joe cut the parts out of wood, "and then from there we just sort of took off with it."

Jackie applied for, and received, a patent on the wooden handbag in the shape of a house and began selling them as a kit. "At first, we sold it flat," she remembers, "and then we found out that women couldn't square things in those days, so Joe would square the box on a frame, glue it together, and then we shipped it with the handles and hinges, the decals for the windows and door, and two colors of Williamsburg paint. I couldn't tell you how many we sold over the years."

The one-and-a-half story handbag house led to this two-story Victorian (right) designed by Susan Sirkis in 1973 using a shell made by Andrews Miniatures. Jackie built the smaller version on the left. Susan's house is half-scale and measures 9"Wx6"Dx12"H. Jackie's version is one-quarter scale, and is 4 1/2"Wx3"Dx6"H. The doll and carriage are both German and the smaller dolls are French.

Jackie took the handbag and some miniature accessories she had made to sell at the regional doll convention in Williamsburg. She also took the miller's house to display and talked Joe into going to the convention with her. "In the beginning, I thought this was girl stuff," Joe insists now, but he soon changed his mind when he saw the miniature furniture for sale there. They were small-size examples of furniture he already knew how to build in full-size. He thought to himself, "Gee, I've made big furniture all my life — this should be a snap," he remembers.

It wasn't, but by then Joe was beginning to be as committed to miniatures as Jackie already was. When they heard that Margaret Whitton would be selling her miniatures business to become a curator at the Margaret Woodbury Strong Museum in Rochester, New York, Jackie called her and arranged to buy the business.

The original inventory of Andrews Miniatures has changed over the years. At first, it consisted of commercial pieces, Joe's handcrafted furniture, and the handbags Jackie had designed. Then Joe began having his designs made in Taiwan and imported to sell in the United States because he could no longer keep up with the demand for the furniture by himself. Eventually Joe had to discontinue his furniture making almost entirely when he lost the use of one eye due to a detached retina that was not diagnosed and treated in time.

Now, Andrews Miniatures represents the work of craftsmen and artisans from all over the United States and sells some commercially-made furniture, too.

Over the years, both Joe and Jackie have been involved in many phases of the miniatures hobby. Both are members of the National Association of Miniature Enthusiasts. Joe was one of the first ten International Miniature Artists chosen in 1978 for his "outstanding contribution to the world of miniatures," and Jackie was elected to N.A.M.E.'s Academy of Honor in 1988. She had served as Secretary of N.A.M.E. from 1978 to 1980, as Junior Vice President from 1980 to 1982, and as a member of N.A.M.E.'s Board of Directors from 1980 to 1986. Jackie had been a founding member of the Virginia Miniature Enthusiasts in 1972, and she is a past president of that group.

In April 1989 Jackie was awarded The Guild Crystal by the International Guild of Miniature Artisans "in recognition of an outstanding contribution throughout the years to the art of miniaturia," according to the citation presented by the Guild. There have been other honors, as well as innumerable hours devoted to promoting the hobby of miniatures.

One of the ways Jackie promotes her hobby is by teaching workshops. She began by conducting a workshop on miniature hat boxes at the N.A.M.E. National Houseparty in 1974, and she has been teaching something to someone ever since. "She is a superb craftsman," her friend and well-known doll artisan Susan Sirkis says about Jackie, "and she can copy anything." Jackie, in turn, believes Susan gave her a valuable hint when she jokingly told Jackie to "fake it, Jack, fake it."

The two have collaborated for years on miniature- and doll-related projects, including a half-scale Victorian dollhouse designed by Susan and built and sold by the Andrewses. Susan insists that Jackie has "an uncanny ability to get people to do what she wants," especially when it comes to the miniature project she might be working on at the moment. "It's a unique talent," Susan believes. Several of the dolls Susan has created are in the Andrews Collection.

Since the early 1970s, the collection has grown primarily in the number of miniature objects it contains. Jackie has made a conscious effort to collect the work of as many of the best contemporary artisans as she can.

She personally prefers replicas of the eighteenth century styles and the currently popular "Country" influence, but she also collects other periods as well.

Many of the artisans represented in Jackie's collection number and date their pieces, and Jackie seems to have quite a few with #13 on them. "I have so many number 13s," she believes, "because some people don't like #13 and I do, so the craftsmen will sell me #13." Isn't she superstitious? "No," she replies firmly, "because I had my first son after two daughters on the thirteenth. How would you feel? Delighted."

She was also delighted when she learned that there would be a book about the collection. "The most thrilling part about this book," Jackie observes, "is not for my living

Jackie uses the souvenirs she collects at each National and Regional N.A.M.E. Houseparty she attends to create a shadow box commemorating each event. These are all from National Houseparties: top, left to right, 1982, 1984, 1983; bottom, left to right, 1985, 1987, 1986.

grandchildren who know the collection, but for future generations to have it." Besides being an overview of the work of artisans currently creating miniatures today, the collection also contains the work of many who have passed away or are simply no longer working in miniature. It is those people who, Jackie feels strongly, should be remembered, and they are represented in her collection. "It will be tomorrow's history," she remarks.

The collection is certainly not static, waiting for tomorrow. Jackie is constantly changing things, adding things. Of her dollhouses, she said: "You never really get through with a house. It's the same as your own. You see something prettier than what you have, so you re-do it." Jackie spends many hours a day working with her miniatures, changing the decor of a house or creating something entirely new. Sometimes that work is devoted to a dollhouse for someone else.

Jackie has recently completed the decoration and furnishings for a fifteen-room dollhouse for Dorothy Stickles, a New York miniatures collector. She had done a smaller, country-style house for her several years ago. Her workroom is adjacent to the rooms containing her collection, so she is never very far from these things she treasures. Jackie says, in fact, that she "could live right here if I just had a bed to sleep on."

Like the child we all wish sometimes we could be, a visit to Jackie Andrews' enchanting collection of dolls, toys, and miniatures makes us believe that it is possible to never "grow up."

Jackie works on the shadow box commemorating the 1988 N.A.M.E. National Houseparty.

Jackie created this hat box (or bandbox) room in 1974 to use as an example in the workshops she taught.

Jackie built and decorated this dining room to display the furniture Joe designed and then had built in Taiwan for sale to Andrews Miniatures' customers in the United States.

The Miller's House

The miller's house was the first miniature house Jackie built. Her son John pulverized real brick from the original house to make the bricks for this chimney.

"This was what was known as the miller's house here in the county," Jackie relates, **"where the man who ran the grinding mill lived."** The house at Rockett Mill in Hanover County, Virginia, had been built in 1735 by Thomas Price. It was located near Patrick Henry's home and served as the general store/post office for the colonists of that time. Its history continued through the American Revolution when Lafayette's troops occupied the building. But it had long since deteriorated when in the late 1960s Jackie decided to build a replica of the historic structure.

The current owner gave Jackie some of the hand-hewn laths from the original building, bricks from the chimney, and stone from the basement to use for the foundation. Jackie had the laths cut by a local lumber yard into the proper size for the one-inch-scale replica, and her son John, then eight years old, carefully pulverized the brick and then molded tiny bricks to use for the chimney of the miniature house.

The original house was built on the side of a hill, so Jackie used papier maché to re-create a landscape for the miniature to sit on. Like its real-size counterpart, the house has a high stone foundation on one side and a porch, which leads into the main rooms of the house and serves as a roof over the entrance to the basement rooms below.

Jackie built the walls of the house by veneering the laths, which had been cut to size, to cardboard. Even the windows were made to look exactly like the ones in the original. "All three sets of windows are different," Jackie points out. "One has nine panes at the top and six on the bottom, one has six on both top and bottom, and one has only four panes."

The miller's house, as created by Jackie Andrews, was the first miniature structure she had ever built, and it was a blue ribbon prize winner when it was first exhibited. "I just had a good time building it," Jackie says simply.

Papier maché was used for the landscaping around the house, and small stones from the basement of the original house provided the foundation.

Since the house sits on a hillside, this porch provides a covered entry to the basement room below. In the mid-1700s, this room in the original house served as a store and post office.

Lakeview

This photo of the real Lakeview was taken in 1966, the same week
Jackie Andrews received the miniature version.

Lakeview was the first dollhouse in Jackie Andrews' collection. It is a copy of Lakeview Farm, the home of Jackie's grandparents, Mr. and Mrs. Charles Luck, on Route 54, west of Ashland, Virginia. Jackie was born and grew up in the house and lived there for a short time after her marriage to Joe Andrews.

The thirteen-room dollhouse was built in 1966 by William Hewlett, an Ashland lumber broker and close friend of the Andrewses. Its overall size is seven feet by eight feet. Bill Hewlett had never built a dollhouse, but he agreed to build one for Jackie after hearing her "fussing about a dollhouse" when the two couples were at a party together. "If you'll shut up, I'll build you a dollhouse," Jackie remembers Bill telling her at the time. At first, Jackie thought she would like to have a replica of a historic dollhouse in a museum, but she couldn't find one for Bill to copy, at least not in the museum in nearby Richmond.

So, Jackie suggested that Bill build her a copy of the house he and his wife, Shirley, lived in. "It was a ranch-type house," Jackie explains, "and I loved that. Bill and Shirley are my very dearest friends, and they thought they'd fox me, so they went to my mother and wanted to copy her house instead. But my mother told them I didn't like her house; the one I really liked was out in the country." So, Bill rode out to Lakeview, and Jackie continues, "He was a person that you could challenge, who would challenge himself to do 'most anything. He took on Lakeview."

During the nine months Bill was building the dollhouse in his basement, Jackie was not allowed to see it, nor did she know that the house was a replica of her childhood home. "I think everybody in town knew," she laughs, "and not a soul told me." When the dollhouse was finished, Shirley Hewlett called to invite Jackie and Joe to a party. Curiously enough, none of Jackie's usual babysitters, her close friends and relatives, including her older children, was available to babysit with John, their youngest child who was then four, on that particular day.

"We went on out to the party," Jackie remembers. "I was standing there watching Shirley fix hors d'oeuvres and just chatting. Bill was leaning on the door frame. I can see him just as plain, and I said, 'Bill, when are you going to let me see my dollhouse?' He replied, 'Well, maybe it's a good time today.' So, we started down the basement steps, and when we got down there, here comes the whole

The miniature version of Lakeview is accurate even to the unusual placement of the second floor windows. Its siding is two layers of cardboard, glued together.

family, mother, children, aunts and uncles, everyone. They were hiding behind the louvers. That's where all my babysitters were, and there, sitting on the floor was Lakeview," she continues, her voice softening. "So, that's always been my love."

Jackie isn't sure when the real Lakeview was built since a courthouse fire destroyed any records kept before 1894, "but my grandfather bought it. It was a small house, and as they continued to have children, they added rooms. In fact, I'm not sure it was originally two stories. I think he pushed the roof up. Mother was born in the downstairs room on the left," Jackie continues, pointing out the corresponding room in the replica, "and in Mother's day they had a governess who lived there. The upstairs room in the left wing was a school room, and the governess had the inside room, which you could enter from the hall."

Jackie has furnished the house in a casual, Country style rather than try to duplicate the furnishings that might have been there during a previous generation. "I probably should have done that schoolroom," she says now, "because so few people in this day and

time know there were such things as live-in governesses."

The dollhouse was originally built enclosed; there was no access from the sides until Jackie's son-in-law, Bill Riggs, "bless his heart, came with a saber saw and cut it open," she recalls. Bill Hewlett had designed the house to be opened by first removing the roof sections to get to the second floor, and then by removing the second floor to get to the first.

According to notes kept by the builder, the following is a parts list for the miniature Lakeview:

> 3,500 total cut parts,
> 414 cut parts in the doors,
> 708 cut parts in the windows,
> 1,892 cut parts in the 22 pairs
>   of window shutters,
> 702 feet of siding material (two layers
>   of cardboard glued together),
> Two 4'x8 1/4' sheets of hardboard
> Five 11'x8 1/8' sheets of hardboard
> 80 ounces of glue,
> 4 spray cans of green paint, and
> 3 quarts of white paint.

Jackie's grandfather enlarged the original house and had the enclosed breezeway built to connect the kitchen (far right) to the rest of the house. "What we called the 'old' kitchen was further back in the yard," she explains, "and that's where all the cooking for the farm hands was done."

"The sentiment attached to it is what really counts," Joe Andrews believes. "He [Bill Hewlett] made everything from scratch. A lot of love went into that house."

Jackie remembers that this living room, on the right as you face the house, used to be her grandparents' bedroom. Now it is furnished as a comfortable country living room with plaid upholstered furniture by Nancy Summers and a bench by Don and Doris Egner. Marjorie Meyer created the flower arrangement, and the schoolhouse quilt on the back wall is counted cross-stitch done by Pamela Andrews. Warren Dick made the child's chair.

Joanna Scarboro built most of the furniture in this kitchen, and Karen Steely made the rug. Harry Scarboro created the butter churn on the floor at the right. Accessories in this room are by Jane Graber, Jim Clark, Elizabeth Chambers, Nancy Elberfeld, Charles Claudon, Gaye Brown, and Vernon Pottery.

Jackie built several of the pieces of furniture in this room from kits, including the red couch in the upstairs hall that can be seen through the bedroom door. Katherine Tinker, an Ashland artisan, created the folk art animals.

**How dear to my heart are the scenes of my childhood,
When fond recollection presents them to view.**
—*Samuel Woodworth*

The Collection Grew . . .

These three views show many of the individual room settings in the collection. The round table in the center is one of four that were in the drug store where Joe and Jackie first met. "This could have been the one I was sitting at when Joe came in," she confides. As a thirty-second wedding anniversary gift, Jackie acquired the table and four chairs from a woman in Ashland who had owned the set since the drug store closed. The original marble table top is stored in the attic, and Jackie has replaced it with a larger wooden top.

**Our desires always increase
with our possessions.**
— *Samuel Johnson*

**The great man is he who does
not lose his child's heart.**
— *Mencius*

*Jackie found this teddy bear parade
(above) at a yard sale. Of German
origin, it is animated by motor-driven
belts. All but one of the bears was
made by Steiff. "I love the baby in
the carriage," Jackie says.*

*This antique dollhouse was probably
built in Albany, New York in 1895.
"The furniture and accessories are
placed according to little notes
written when the house was packed
away," Jackie says.*

A blue story-and-a-half, late Victorian cottage sits below a wall hanging "Grandma's Front Porch," created by Fred Cobb.

Jackie bought this house from Barbara's Mini World in 1979 and has yet to finish it. "It doesn't have any wallpaper; it doesn't have any moldings," she admits. "It's got a long way to go."

A Märklin train from Germany surrounds this vignette. Barbara Jones created the bed, and Joanna Scarboro added the pillows. Paula Watkins made the red teddy bear, and David Krupick created the wooden toy under the signpost. The rocking horse is a Hallmark collectible, and the alphabet blocks spell out Jackie's name.

The largest rocking horse is a commercial product, but the tiny ones just underneath were created by Jackie's daughter, Cecile Cox. The one on the left is an antique, and some of the others were created by Jackie, Ted Norton, Dick Austin, Dorothy Midgett, Betty Jensen, and The Doll Peddlar.

The doll centering this photograph is a Colleen Moore dollhouse doll, surrounded by three antique metal wagons, two commercially-made wagons, and a handcrafted wooden one. The black baby doll is by Beverly Parker, the apples in the basket are by Cecile Cox, and Retta Hughes did the picnic basket.

Martha Sewell made the two black dolls, whose heads are wooden balls, and even though it hardly ever snows in Virginia, there are quite a few sleds in Jackie's collection, as well as assorted winter hats, scarves, and a sweater.

Wilton

When Jackie Andrews bought the Wilton dollhouse in 1977, it was considered an adventure in creative financing. Jackie went to see Mr. Will Buchanan, Jr., then Assistant Cashier and manager of the Ashland branch of the First & Merchants Bank, a family friend "whom I had known since he was this high," Jackie recalls with a gesture of her hand. "I said that I wanted to borrow some money for a house in Williamsburg, and he asked how much money did I need?" she continues. Fifteen thousand dollars was the answer. Then he asked, " 'Is that all you need to buy a house in Williamsburg?' and I said, 'Yes, it's a dollhouse.' Well," she laughs, "his mouth went open like that."

The loan application was taken to the bank's lending committee for approval. "The way he compared it," Jackie explains, "was the time they loaned money to a farmer on a sow's unborn pigs. That was the gamble they took." But, the bank approved a five-year mortgage on the dollhouse, pending an appraisal which was done by two knowledgeable historians from Colonial Williamsburg.

This transaction, believed to be the first dollhouse ever with a mortgage of its own, made headlines around the country. And, five years later, when the final monthly installment was paid, *The National Enquirer* added to the dollhouse's notoriety by publishing a photograph of Jackie and Joe Andrews with an officer from the bank, participating in the burning of the Wilton mortgage papers.

The dollhouse is a one-inch-scale replica of the real Wilton, which was built in 1753 by William Randolph III. It stands fifty inches tall, is sixty-seven inches wide and forty-six inches deep, and it has eight rooms

on two floors — four on the front facade, four on the back — and center hallways on both floors that run the entire depth of the house.

The idea for the Wilton dollhouse was conceived by Mrs. Owen (Betty) Smith of Williamsburg, Virginia, who got the plans for the original house from The Colonial Dames of America, and commissioned Robert Simms, Conservator of Furniture at Colonial Williamsburg, to build the shell, a six-year part-time project. The walls are carved wood blocks painted grey with white trim to resemble the original house's brick exterior. The roof is covered with 5,000 slate-colored Formica shingles, which Owen Smith cut and applied. All of the windows in the house are operable and have muntins on each side of the glass — a total of 1,000 tiny sticks of wood, which Mr. Smith cut to fit exactly. The individual panes of glass are made from old microscope slides and have the wavy appearance of handmade, eighteenth-century glass.

The Smiths spent a full year building the four chimneys for the dollhouse. Each is made of wood, painted with a mortar mixture, and faced with 6,160 tiny bricks, which were made of real brick dust and laid in bond.

The late Richard Mann of Charlottesville, Virginia, made the majority of the furniture for the dollhouse while the Smiths owned it. Some items were copied from pieces in the Henry Ford Museum in Dearborn, Michigan. Jackie has since made some minor changes in the furnishings, adding rugs and some individual pieces of furniture to several of the rooms. "It did not have but one rug when I bought it," she remarks.

Marjorie Brandt stitched three of the rugs — "all but the blue Chinese." Jackie points out. "Mitzy Van Horn did that one. She did a lot of the brass, the locks on the doors. I think she is one of the greatest craftswomen of *any* time." Jackie herself did the rug in the lower hallway. "My one piece of needlework," she confirms, "and I was drunk when I did it. I had broken my arm and leg, and they kept giving me Darvocet which went straight to my head. So, not a stitch runs straight like everybody says they are supposed to," she insists. "They run at a slant."

Pointing out the bed coverings in one of the Wilton bedrooms, Jackie explains that they are silk embroidery thread on a delicate silk fabric. The bed coverings were handpainted when Jackie bought the house, because "Betty couldn't find anyone to do needlework when they did the house, but she could find someone who painted." Jackie took the bed coverings off and sent them to Jean Strup, a miniature needlework artist in Florida, who duplicated the painted design in silk thread. She also created the window treatments, a dressing table and stool, and the seat covering on one of the chairs in that room.

The dollhouse has both a front and back facade which are stored away, and the openings are now covered with Plexiglas so each room can be viewed more easily.

In keeping with its elegant Georgian architecture, the Wilton dollhouse is furnished in a style typical of the 1750s period when the original house was first occupied by the Randolphs. A tour of this exceptional miniature house gives the viewer a real sense of how a wealthy early Virginia family might have lived.

Betty Valentine created the wing chair in this drawing room, and many of the other pieces of furniture are by Richard Mann and original to the house. The harpsichord is a copy of one in the Governor's Palace in Williamsburg. Roger Steinbach created the violin and fireplace brass.

Richard Mann's furniture fills the dining room. Barbara Epstein made the porcelain dishes in the cupboard, and the soup tureen was made by Deborah McKnight. The silver is by Eugene Kupjack, and Mitzi Van Horn did the needlepoint rug.

Richard Mann also made several of the pieces of furniture in this library. The nested tables are by Eric Pearson, the card table is from Willoughby Studio, and Roger Gutheil made the brown leather chair for Chestnut Hill. Mitzi Van Horn did the needlework on the chaise and firescreen and made the brass candlesticks. The ship model is by George Becker, and Barbara Cosgrove designed the rug, which was stitched by Marjorie Brandt.

The table in this kitchen was made by Robert Simms, and the high chair and hutch were made by Richard Mann. The chairs around the table are English and were made in 1972. Mitzi Van Horn made the fireplace tools and hanging light fixture. Jackie points out the silver porringer on the high chair and says of Wilton's builder and first owner, "Betty told me this is where they always fed the baby, and he always ate off sterling silver. She had marvelous stories to tell about the house."

Over my slumber your loving watch keep—
Rock me to sleep, mother;
Rock me to sleep.

—*Elizabeth Akers Allen*

The chest at the foot of the Hepplewhite bed in the child's bedroom is by Roger Steinbach. Richard Mann made the painted chest and cradle, and the writing arm Windsor is by Edward Norton. Betty Valentine made the child-sized chair, and Owen Smith created the toys.

Harry Cooke made the arm chair in the center of this Queen Anne-style bedroom, and Betty Valentine made the wing chair. All of the other furniture is by Richard Mann. Jean Strup did the silk-on-silk embroidery on the bed hangings, draperies, dressing table, and stool.

Note these examples of intricate silk embroidery by needlework artist Jean Strup.

This Chippendale-style bedroom is furnished as if it might have belonged to Peyton Randolph, the owner of the original Wilton, with furniture by Richard Mann. Mitzi Van Horn created the bed hangings, the rug, and the 18th-century clothing. The wing chair is by Betty Valentine.

The Sheraton-style bedroom has furniture by Richard Mann. The bed posts and dressing table have reeded detailing.

A Charles Claudon cat seems to look longingly at the contents of this birdcage by Laurel Coulon. Nancy Van Horn created the needlework covering for the stool from Andrews Miniatures. The chest and shaving stand with mirror were made by Gerald Crawford.

Oriental Expressions

The doll on the left is a porcelain, articulated Japanese, and the three on the right are wooden. The doll in the box at the center has a selection of ceremonial wigs. The glass case and house in the front are Chinese, and the miniature tilt-top table was painted by Betty Spice.

These small Oriental vendor stands range in size from 2"x4 1/2" to 3"x6" and were made in Japan, but not for export. They were brought to this country by a friend of Jackie's after a tour of duty in Japan with the U.S. Army.

Kitchen Collectibles

This Nuremberg kitchen was made about 1890 and is 24 3/4"Wx13"H. These kitchens were made for little girls as educational toys. Everything that was needed for a household and its maintenance was usually reproduced in miniature.

This black doll is an advertisement for Aunt Jemima pancake mix. The doll-sized stove is marked "Favorite," and the ice box has a tin tub inside. The half-scale black stove is actually a pencil sharpener.

Jason Getzan made the copper items shown on the top of an antique stove.

Jackie made the hutch, which is filled with an assortment of mostly German pottery and porcelain. Of the three chairs, the largest one is a German antique, the middle one is an early dollhouse chair, and the smallest one is by Warren Dick. Robert Bernhard made the folding screen, and the dish filled with fruit is Nippon from Japan.

This doll's tea set has gold trim with a blue-and-pink flower pattern, but it is unmarked. The miniature set in the center is Blue Willow by Deborah McKnight.

I know well that happiness is in little things.

— John Ruskin

Jackie bought this antique walnut table in 1972. It sits on a braided rug made of dyed silk stockings. The two books are THE CHIMES, published by Oxford University, and a book of French proverbs. The other accessories on the table are metal and are probably of German origin. Gerald Crawford made the miniature round table.

Peter Acquisto made this silver service for Jackie in 1984. The tray is 1 7/8 inches long and 7/8 inches wide. An Ashland, Virginia, jeweler hand-engraved Jackie's monogram on all four pieces.

A Country Cottage

Jackie calls this small house "one of my pets." She built most of the furniture in it from kits, which, she insists, "is the only way I can build furniture." The house has a casual, country ambiance.

Is not a small house best?...
—Ralph Waldo Emerson

Jackie made the settle bench, couch, coffee table, and the table in the corner from kits. She made the hutch in a workshop taught by George and Sally Hoffman, and Gerald Crawford made the arm chair. The painting over the fireplace was created by George Schlosser, and the goose in the window is by Frank Balestrieri. Don Hanky made the two canvas-back ducks, and the picnic basket was woven by John Fleming. The rug in this room came from Sherwood Interiors.

The kitchen cupboards were all made by Jackie
from kits, and Paul Rouleau built the pie safe. The
blue sugar bin in the back of this room is by Bruce
Bantle, and John Moffatt made the straight chair on
the right. Accessories were made by a variety of
craftsmen, including Frances Steak, Elizabeth
Chambers, Jane Graber, Tom Thumb and Gail Wise.

Jackie made this four-poster bed from a kit, and then found that it was too tall for the room. "So I had to take off that much," she laughs, holding up finger and thumb to indicate about an inch and a half, "and I just went on and made a stool." The little stool she is referring to is on the right. Betty Valentine made the child's chair, and Al Chandronnait created the painted box. The cattails are by Rosemary Dyke, the grey cat is by Jacki Transue, Bonnie Bennett made the penny wooden doll, and the teddy bear was created by Cynthia Barron. Karen Steely did the checkerboard on the painted chest against the back wall.

A Carolina Cabin 🏠

Ron and April Gill built this rustic Carolina cabin.

Jackie landscaped and furnished the yard behind the cabin, a task she claims not to enjoy. "I don't like outdoor work in big or little," she insists. "Flowers don't grow for me."

The side of the cabin opens to reveal the main first floor rooms, as well as a bedroom tucked up under the roof where two Beverly Parker dolls seem to be just waking up. Jackie points out that the cat has had kittens in the cradle because "it no longer has any other use." Laura Gill made most of the furniture for this house.

Christic Church 🏠

Dr. Charles E. Holcomb, builder of the Carter's Grove replica, also built this miniature version of Christ Church near Irvington, in Lancaster County, Virginia, for Mrs. Betty Carter Marvin. At the time she commissioned it, Mrs. Marvin intended to give it to the church as a gift. When it turned out that the church did not have the space to display the replica, she offered it to the Andrews instead.

Like Carter's Grove, the real church has a close connection to the Carter family. In 1730, Robert "King" Carter agreed to provide the funds to replace an old church originally built on the site by his father, John Carter, if two conditions were met: if the church could be built on the same site as the first, and if the vestry agreed to allow the chancel to continue to be a burial place for his family. Carter died in 1732, so he never saw the finished structure. Completed in 1734, Christ Church is believed to be the oldest Episcopal church in the United States which still has its original furnishings.

Christ Church is cruciform in style, built in a shape similar to a Greek cross, and its three-feet-thick brick walls are set in the Flemish bond pattern. Much of the interior wood-

work is walnut, including the three-decker pulpit with its carved sounding board above which is inlaid with pine. Three-decker pulpits were typical in Colonial churches. The minister read the service from the middle desk and gave the sermon from the upper level.

Christ Church is considered an architectural gem, although no one is certain who designed it. Many architectural historians believe that it was designed by Sir Christopher Wren, and others believe that if it was not, at least by someone who had studied under him. In any case, the real Christ Church is now a registered national historic landmark, open to the public and administered by Grace Episcopal Church in nearly Kilmarnock.

This replica of Christ Church is a truly unique addition to the Andrews collection, and Jackie plans to fill it with dolls representing the Tidewater Virginia families who originally worshipped in the real church. "The interior is really more interesting to me than Carter's Grove," Joe comments about the carved wood paneling and the unique interior appointments of this replica.

These interior views of Christ Church show the raised pulpit, enclosed pews, and lovely wood-work. In cruciform churches such as this one, the pulpit was placed at one of the re-entrant angles of the crossing. In Christ Church it is at the re-entrant angle on the south. There are twenty-six high-backed, enclosed pews in the church. Typically, each pew was assigned to a family who either bought or rented it.

Vintage Victorian 🏠

This Victorian dollhouse, built by Richard Kempson of New Jersey, almost didn't get into the collection at all. While en route to Virginia to deliver the dollhouse to Jackie, Mr. Kempson exhibited the dollhouse at a miniatures show in a motel that caught fire. According to Jackie, "He kept going back in, and the firemen kept fussin' at him, and he said, 'I've got to get my house out of there,' so he brought it out in pieces and put it on the sidewalk."

As in many of her houses, Jackie did the interior decorating herself. "I worked one whole Sunday doing the windows at the back," she says, "so I could put the mirror between them." The table and two chairs at the front of this room are by Betty Valentine. The small marble-top table on the left was made by Nic Nichols and holds a lamp by Leonard and Kathy Schiada. Susan Snodgrass and Stephanie Blythe made the centerpiece on the large round table in the center of the room, which is one of the four Belter-style pieces of furniture by Stan Lewis in this room. The porcelain is by Laurel Coulon, and Marjorie Brandt stitched the rug.

Verl Kraeger made the furniture in this dining room, and the dishes on the table are by Paul McNeely.

The red sofa and wing chair in this upstairs sitting room were made by Mell Prescott. Verl Kraeger made the table next to the wing chair, which has on it an arrangement by Mary Payne. The bird cage is by Laurel Coulon.

Illusion is the first of all pleasures.
— *Voltaire*

Nancy Summers made the larger pieces of furniture in this bedroom, including the bed, and Mary Hoot created the fabric cat on top. Suzanne Russo built the swan chair, and Marjorie Brandt stitched the rug.

Bettyanne Twigg created this Victorian bedroom, which is a room box and not a part of the yellow Victorian house shown on page 64. She designed the patterns for curtains, draperies, bed coverings, and the table skirt. The lamp and dresser set are from Chrysnbon, and the furniture is commercially made.

*This pink Victorian was built by Ron and April Gill. They
also provided the landscaped setting around the house,
installed the lighting, and papered and painted the interior.
"They are very gifted people," Jackie points out.*

Laura Gill built the cupboards in this kitchen, which has a simulated tin ceiling. Some of the accessories were created by Deborah McKnight, Roberta Partridge, and Sylvia Clark.

In the attic carefully lined in newspapers by the Gills, are trunks by Suzanne Russo, a mattress from Dawn Weaver, and a quilt made by Vivian Puckett.

Holiday Traditions

This dollhouse, designed by Joe Andrews, was modeled after an English house, circa 1850, and measures 14"Wx13"Dx22"H. Its simulated brick facade provides the background for a selection of wreaths and other holiday decorations from Jackie's collection.

**Variety's the very spice of life,
That gives it all its flavour.**

— *William Cowper*

The wreath and swag shown here were created by Mary Payne. Chet Spacher made the brass candlesticks, and Mary McGrath created the cardinal sculpture.

This Christmas wreath is studded with tiny lights and centered with a charming Santa scene. Cecile Cox created the tree, and Jackie made the setting and dressed the Santa doll. In fact, she made a total of thirty of the wreaths, which are now in collections all over the country.

Close-up of Santa room on facing page.

Jackie has a round, wooden cake stand in the center of her special "drug store" table, which she changes with the seasons and holidays. This setting is the one she uses at Christmas-time. Among the many accessories shown are an elf by Cynthia Barron, a stack of packages by Julie Wheeler, and a plate of cookies by Deborah McKnight. The punch tray and cookies on the table are by Edna Bishop.

**Heap high the board with plenteous cheer,
and gather to the feast...**
— Alice Williams Brotherton

Joe Andrews built this dining table, and the chairs are from Andrews Miniatures. Susan Sirkis created the black maid, and the butler is an antique German doll. All of the food is porcelain and was made by Deborah McKnight. Joan Durigg made the little girl in the white dress.

Not believe in
Santa Claus?
You might as well
not believe
in fairies...
— *Francis P. Church*

Beverly Walters made the head of this large Santa doll, which was assembled and dressed by Martha Sewell. The decorated tree on the left was created by Jo Cockrell, and the one on the right by Margaret O'Halloran. Joe Andrews designed the table, produced in Taiwan, which holds the Spode Christmas dishes by Jo Parker and a Williamsburg centerpiece Jackie made in a workshop taught by Roberta Partridge.

Holiday Traditions

"Country Critters' Christmas" is a room box setting created by Nancy Elberfeld in 1985.

The filled stockings hung against this Braxton Payne fireplace were a gift to Jackie from Judy Berman. Gail Morey created the dogs, and the andirons were made by Chet Spacher.

Ron and April Gill created this winter front-porch setting for a Christmas caroling vignette. Carol Boyd made the eleven dolls in the scene, including a baby in a sleigh made by Carol Hardy. Chet Spacher created the lamp post.

This Halloween table top includes an assortment of autumn accessories. The flat tray of cookies is by Pam Gibson, and the carved pumpkin in front was made by Robin Betterley. Edna Bishop created a tray of pumpkin cookies, the apple-bobbing dish, and the cider on the table.

Easter is celebrated with rabbits, both old and new. Several of the baskets were created by Margaret O'Halloran, Roberta Partridge, and Cecile Cox. The egg coloring essentials are by Small Thoughts by Dawn. The larger eggs are papier maché; the smaller ones are tin.

Edward Norton's desk holds glassware by Francis Whittemore and delicate valentines in their boxes from Bernice Stevens. Appropriately, Betty Valentine made the chair.

Jackie designed and built these two houses, stacked one on top of the other, to display all the Chrysnbon kits and accessories. The upper house has a red decor, and the lower one is blue. The small houses in the shelf unit at the left are ceramic. On top of the Chrysnbon houses are an Andrews house handbag and a golf vignette, which, Jackie points out with amusement, shows a squirrel in the tree with the missing golf ball.

This view of the red Chrysnbon house shows the sewing room on the upper floor with a portion of the nursery on the left and a glimpse into the bathroom on the right.

The dining room in the red Chrysnbon house features Chrysnbon furniture, all made from highly detailed, wood-grained polystyrene kits.

Classic Colonial 🏠

A striped sofa Jackie made is at the front of this living room. The wing chairs were made by Betty Valentine, and Annelle Ferguson stitched the firescreen. The handsome desk on the left side of the room was handpainted by Dorothy Midgett. All the fireplace brass was made by Chet Spacher, and Deborah McKnight created the porcelain bowl. Jackie made the two Chippendale mirrors flanking the fireplace, and the painting above the mantel was done by Catherine B. MacLaren, the Founding Editor of NUTSHELL NEWS. Jackie considers the painting "a real treasure."

This Colonial dollhouse was built by Marion Howes in 1977. It has eight rooms with a center hallway on each floor, and Jackie has decorated it in classic eighteenth-century style, using Williamsburg blue as the central color.

Joe Andrews built the dining table, chairs, and the lowboys in this dining room. Edward Norton constructed the corner cupboards, and the rug was made by Marjorie Brandt. The room also contains a flower arrangement by Wilma Thomas, Deborah McKnight's porcelain, and knife boxes by Delores Rawding. Jean Yingling made the porcelain fruit bowl. The silver is by Peter Acquisto, Eugene Kupjack, Cini, and several pieces were made in Colonial Williamsburg.

In a small sitting room on the second floor, the wing chair was made by d. Anne Ruff and re-upholstered by Jackie. Hank Taylor built the lingerie chest, and the sewing basket beside the chair was done by Frank Morley. The bathroom fixtures that can be seen through the open door were an early Houseparty souvenir.

The furniture in this child's bedroom was made by Jim Hillhouse and painted by his wife, Shirley. The toys are by Barbara and Lew Kummerow, and Mary Hoot's cat sits at the foot of the bed.

This room box, titled "Only Two Weeks....1969–1982," is an unusually accurate replica of the kitchen in Jackie's apartment on the college campus. It was created by Jeannette Ewing, who worked with Jackie. A gift to Jackie, it commemorates the fact that Jackie, who thought she was being hired as night supervisor at the college infirmary for "only two weeks," is still there.

Jackie built and furnished this replica of a den in one of the early homes in Hanover County, Virginia, called "Cool Water." The decorator who had done the full-sized room saw the miniature Jackie had created and recognized it immediately. Jackie used balsa wood to make the brick floor and laid each piece individually. She used scraps of the original fabric for the draperies and carefully copied each of the three doors in the room, which have three different types of paneling.

"Famous Fido's Doggie Deli" was designed and created by Gail Morey in 1984, after a photograph in PEOPLE magazine. The building was constructed by Donald Tuttle. "I liked it right from the beginning," Joe remarks, "and then after we bought it, I couldn't wait to take it out to Chicago to show it to the woman who had the real delicatessen. She was thrilled with what she saw. These are the things that I get a big kick out of," he adds.

Inside "Famous Fido's Doggie Deli" by Gail Morey.

Gail Morey also created this pool room and filled it with her dogs in human-like poses.

Ron and April Gill built this half-scale tarpaper shack. The doll on the left is a Louisiana mud fishing lady, and the three small dolls are china. The mammy doll on the front porch is metal and the man doll is cloth. Jackie made the large mammy doll, holding a German bisque baby, out of wire armature and used a black walnut for a head.

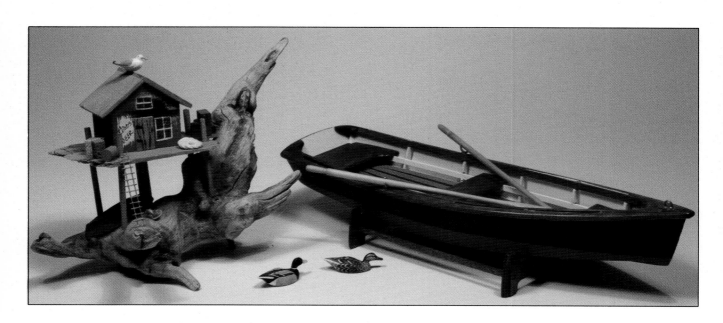

Hank Taylor made this boat, and Frank Balestrieri created the ducks.
Jackie found the driftwood sculpture at a craft show.

These views of Boot Hill Cemetery are part of a larger vignette created by members of a California miniatures group in 1984 and given to Jackie by Joanna Scarboro. The animals, vultures, and the minister were made by Maxine Smith.

Doorways of

Handcrafted Treasures

Harry Cooke is one of the superb furniture craftsmen whose work Jackie believes she is privileged to own. In early 1979, as Jackie remembers it, "I was trying to collect a piece from each of the first ten members of International Miniature Artists (now the Academy of Honor), and I had not succeeded in getting anything by Harry Cooke." So she went to a show where she knew he would be exhibiting his work. "As good luck would have it, I was right at the entrance where every dealer had to come in. When I saw him come through the door," she continues, "I said, 'Mr. Cooke, I want to buy a piece of furniture.'" He told Jackie that he only had three pieces for sale that day, a corner cupboard, a breakfront, and a chair. "I said I'd take the chair," Jackie remembers.

"I thought anybody can afford to buy a chair." When the show opened, Jackie went straight to his table to look at the chair. "I asked him the price, and he said $400. I gulped, but I said I'd take it. Then he said, 'Oh, wait a minute. I've got this little chest with me, and that's for sale, too.'" When Jackie asked the price, she found that it was $400, too. After a few moments hesitation, she decided to buy both the pieces and says today, "They are my treasures. The chair is a classic Pennsylvania chair, and it does not have a straight line in it," she points out. The bombe chest, dated 1977, is complete even to the tiny screws and nuts that hold the drawer pulls in place. Amanda Skinner created the Chinese Export porcelain shown on top of the chest.

The loom on the left was made by Ron Stetkewicz. Warren Dick made the loom on the right and the flax wheel. A selection of quilts and woven coverlets from the collection includes the bear's paw quilt Jackie made from a kit. "I had never done a quilt before in my life, and I'll never do another one," Jackie laughs.

In this furniture grouping, Hermania Anslinger created the sofa and table. The columnar stand on the left is by Natasha Beshenkovsky, and the other one is by Roy Augustine. The silver bowl is by Eugene Kupjack, and Amanda Skinner created the Rose Medallion bowl. Chet Spacher made the candlestick, and Mary Payne created the arrangement of dogwood.

*This "Fish 'N Bait" house is one of a kind,
built by Chet Spacher.*

*These are two of the three fruit
and vegetable stands in the
collection. The one on the left is
by Small Thoughts by Dawn,
signed and dated 1981. Jackie
built the one on the right from a
kit at the N.A.M.E. National
Houseparty in Atlanta in 1987.*

Jackie bought this "Swimming Hole" vignette, created by Dawn Adams, because it reminded her of the place she went swimming near her childhood home, "although we were never allowed to 'skinny,'" she insists.

This photograph was on the cover of the only catalog published by Andrews Miniatures, which came out in 1975.

Miniatures on these shelves include some of the tiny houses Jackie collects, a selection of round tables and accessories for various holidays and seasons, and other furniture and accessories that will be used in future room boxes or dollhouses. On the shelves below are some of the research material, books, and magazines relating to Jackie's various collections.

The china-head doll was made in Germany, as was the white dog next to her and the antique opera glasses. Susan Sirkis created the table, and the flower arrangement is by Barbara Meyer. Martha Farnsworth made the pillow and the corset, and the basket came from Small Ideas. Wilma Thomas made the gloves, and Julie Wheeler created the ornaments and packages.

Jackie made this striped sofa in the early 1970s. Sharon Garmize designed and stitched the tray, and the needlework dolls were done by Martha Farnsworth. Annelle Ferguson created the sampler.

A delicate bedspread by Vivian Puckett is the background for an assortment of fantasy accessories. The fairy crown was created by Susan Snodgrass and Stephanie Blythe, and the set of jewelry on a white square is by Jean Bodine. There is a diamond in the center of the pearl and green jewelry box by Eugene Kupjack , and the other jewelry shown was created by Carolyn Gray. Brooke Tucker made the set of luggage.

Jackie marvels that the afghan of granny squares by Jean Gibson is "light as a feather." The spool cabinet is from Jean Schroeder's Dollhouse World.

Moving Day

Like many other American households, the Andrews Collection also occasionally experiences the upheaval of moving day. Let's pretend that the moving van has just left, and our miniature homeowners must find space in their new home for the following: two paintings by Betty Spice and Mary Lou Laughon, a Natasha Beshenkovsky chest with Bill Robertson's tea caddy, a Terry Rogel table with silver by Obadiah Fisher, and a wing chair by Robert Bernhard, with Ernest Levy's tea caddy on its seat. There are also two six-board chests, the one on the bottom by Don Buttfield, with Cliff Haas's on top. Therese Bahl created the painted chest, and the hanging shelf is by Hank Taylor. Gay Lyon made the rush-seated arm and side chairs, Jeanette Vines upholstered the square-cushioned chair, and Hal Weston built the armoire. There are even some Rosemary Dyke flowers to welcome this family to their new home.

One of the half-inch-scale items in the collection is this house by Bauder Pine, which is a copy of the Tully Smith house in Atlanta. The pie safe in front, by Paul Rouleau, is a copy of one in the original house. Other half-scale furniture is by Susan Hoeltge, Betty Valentine, Susy Q, Nancy Summers, Mell Prescott, and other pieces by Paul Rouleau. Harry Scarboro made the butter churn, and Chet Spacher created the brass pieces. The cat is by Jacki Transue.

To all, to each,
    a fair good-night,
And pleasing dreams,
    and slumbers light.
    —*Sir Walter Scott*

Jackie's collection contains dozens of these replica houses by Mott Miniatures, which were originally offered in three different sizes.

Joe was lucky enough to win this lovely nursery room box at a N.A.M.E. National Houseparty in Rochester, New York, in 1983. Joe bought ten dollars worth of tickets, Jackie recalls, and told her, "I'm going to win that." Although she doubted he would, she was very pleased that he did win, and the room has become a charming addition to the Andrews Collection.

Index to Artisans and Craftsmen

Jackie and Joe Andrews invite you to visit their collection in person. It is located in Ashland, Virginia, north of Richmond at exit #39 of I-95, and can be seen by appointment. For an appointment to view the collection, call Jackie Andrews at (804) 798-8186, or write to her at P.O. Box 707, Ashland, Va. 23005.

Like Jackie Andrews, Anne Day Smith is also a collector; she still has her childhood dollhouse.

Anne has been writing professionally since high school. For the past dozen years, she has been a freelance writer/photographer specializing in miniatures and a regular contributing editor to *Nutshell News*. Her articles have also appeared in several newspapers and other magazines.

Anne is the author of two previous books focusing on the miniatures hobby: *Interior Design in Miniature*, featuring the work of Brooke Tucker, published in 1986; and *Masters in Miniature*, featuring the work of twelve different contemporary artisans, published in 1987.

Anne and her husband, Gerry, have three grown sons and have just moved to their restored 18th-century home in Maine.